TWITTER MARKETING WORKBOOK: HOW TO USE TWITTER FOR BUSINESS

2016 EDITION

BY JASON MCDONALD, PH.D.

© 2015-2016, JM INTERNET GROUP

https://www.jm-seo.org/

Tel. 800-298-4065

0

INTRODUCTION

Welcome to the *Twitter Marketing Workbook, 2016 edition*! Get ready to

- have some **fun**;
- **learn how Twitter works;**
- understand how to use **Twitter** to **market your business**; and
- create a step-by-step **Twitter marketing plan**.

Fully revised and updated for 2016, this workbook not only explains how to market on Twitter but also provides access to **free** Twitter marketing tools. It provides overviews, step-by-step instructions, tips and secrets, free tools for Twitter marketing, and (*wait, there's more!*) access to worksheets that will help you build a systematic Twitter marketing plan. Even better, if you register your copy, you also get access to my complete *Social Media Toolbook*, with literally hundreds of free social media marketing tools to turbocharge your social media marketing not just on Twitter but also on LinkedIn, Facebook, YouTube, Google+, Instagram and other major social media platforms.

> *It slices, it dices. It explains how to Twitter works. It gives you free tools. And it helps you make a Twitter marketing plan.*

If you're really gung-ho for **social media marketing**, I refer you to my *Social Media Workbook*, an all-in-one guide to the entire social media universe from Twitter to LinkedIn, Twitter to YouTube, Instagram to Pinterest, Yelp to Google+, and everything in between. Learn more about that book at http://jmlinks.com/social or call 800-298-4065.

Why Market via Twitter?

If you've read this far, you're definitely intrigued by Twitter as a marketing platform. Perhaps you're just starting out with a **Twitter Account** for your **business**. Or perhaps you already have a Twitter account, but want to make it really work. Let's step back for a minute and ask: **why market on Twitter**?

Here are some reasons:

- **Twitter is big.** Twitter is among the largest social media platforms with 235 million users.
- **Twitter is timely.** Twitter is the "goto" place for breaking news, including specific industry news at industry trade shows and when something new happens in your industry.
- **Twitter is targeted.** Yes, there's a lot of pop culture on Twitter, but Twitter has specific micro uses such as coupons, special deals, insider loyalty programs for your best customers. If you know how to zero in, you may find amazing niche opportunities hidden inside the Twitter blizzard of pop culture noise.
- **Twitter is free**. Twitter is, of course, free to use. And in terms of marketing there is a lot you can do, for free, to build your brand, spread eWOM (electronic word of mouth), help you stay top-of-mind with your customers, and drive real people to your retail store or small business website.
- **Twitter May Not Be for You**. Twitter has an enormous hype factory behind it, and many marketers are terrified if they are not on Twitter, they're missing out. As a small businessperson, you may also feel "Twitter guilt," the feeling that you should be on Twitter but don't know how. However, after researching Twitter and understanding how Twitter really works, you may discover that it really isn't for you. Knowing that Twitter is not for you based on systematic research can save you a lot of time, time you can devote to other social media that do work for your business. "No," as they say is the second best answer (after "Yes").
- **Twitter has advertising.** If you advertise smart on Twitter, and combine paid advertising with free organic Twitter marketing, you can target not only your current customers but also prospective customers based on interests, thereby radically extending the reach of your online marketing efforts. You can even target specific journalists via Twitter!

Twitter, however, is also complicated. Using it is one thing, and marketing on Twitter is another. Most businesses fail at Twitter marketing because they just don't "get it." They don't understand how Twitter works, and they fail to see the incredible marketing opportunities drowned out by the blizzard of pop culture on Twitter. Twitter is also not user-friendly, with its own lingo, codes, and etiquette. You first have to find out if your customers are on Twitter, and then have to create a laser-focused Twitter marketing strategy.

Quite simply, you have to invest some time to learn "how" to market on Twitter.

Enter the *Twitter Marketing Workbook*.

Who is this Workbook For?

This workbook is aimed primarily at **small business owners** and **marketing managers**. Non-profits will also find it useful.

If you are a person whose job involves advertising, marketing, and/or branding, this workbook is for you. If you are a small business that sees a marketing opportunity in Twitter, this workbook is for you. And if your job is to market a business or organization online in today's Internet economy, this book is for you. Anyone who wants to look behind the curtain and understand the mechanics of how to market on Twitter will benefit from this book.

- Anyone who sees – however dimly – that Twitter could help market their business will benefit from this hands-on guide.
- Anyone who is mystified by Twitter, yet would like to know for sure if it might work as a marketing method will benefit from this hands-on guide.

How Does This Workbook Work?

This workbook starts first with an overview to **social media *marketing***. If social media is a **party**, then **using social media** is akin to just *showing up*. **Marketing** on social media, in contrast, isn't about showing up. It's about ***throwing*** the party!

Understanding that distinction between "attending" the social media party and "throwing" the social media party is the subject of **Chapter One.**

Chapter Two is a deep dive into Twitter marketing. We'll overview how Twitter works, explain everything from accounts to tweets, @ signs to #hashtags, and even why you might put a "dot" in front of an "@" sign on Twitter. It will all become much clearer, as we work through Twitter in plain English, written for "mere mortals." Along the way, I'll provide **worksheets** that will act as "Jason as therapist," so you can fill them out and begin to outline your own unique Twitter marketing plan.

Finally, this workbook ends with an **Appendix**: a list of amazing **free Twitter tools** and resources. Even better, if you register your copy, you get clickable online access to the tools, a PDF copy of the book, and (wait, there's more!) a complimentary copy of my *Social Media Toolbook*, my compilation of hundreds of social media tools not just for Twitter but for all the major platforms.

Here's how to register your copy of this workbook:

1. Go to https://jm-seo.org/workbooks
2. Click on Twitter.
3. Use this password: **twitter2016**
4. You're in. Simply click on the link for a PDF copy of the *Social Media Toolbook* as well as access to the worksheets referenced herein.

OK, now that we know what this workbook is about, who it is for, and our plan of action...

Let's get started!

≫ MEET THE AUTHOR

My name is Jason McDonald, and I have been active on the Internet since 1994 (having invented the Internet along with Al Gore) and taught SEO, AdWords, and Social Media since 2009 – online, at Stanford University Continuing Studies, at both AcademyX and the Bay Area Video Coalition in San Francisco, at workshops, and in corporate trainings across these United States. I love figuring out how things work, and I love teaching others! Social media marketing is an endeavor that I understand, and I want to empower you to understand it as well.

Learn more about me at https://www.jasonmcdonald.org/ or at my corporate website https://www.jm-seo.org/. Or just call 800-298-4065, say something flattering, and I my secretary will put you through. *(Like I have a secretary! Just call if you have something to ask or say).*

≫ SPREAD THE WORD: WRITE A REVIEW & GET A FREE eBOOK!

If you like this workbook, please take a moment to write an honest review on Amazon.com. *If you hate the book, feel free to trash it on Amazon or anywhere across the Internet. (I have thick skin). If you hate life, in general, and are just one of those bitter people who write bitter reviews... well, gosh, go off and meditate, talk to a priest or do something spiritual. Life is just too short to be that bitter!*

At any rate, here is my special offer for those lively enough to write a review of the book–

1. Write your **honest review** on Amazon.com.
2. **Contact** me via https://www.jm-seo.org/contact and let me know your review is up.
3. Include your **email address** and **website URL**, and any quick questions you have about it.
4. I will send you a **free** copy of one of my other eBooks which cover AdWords, SEO, and Social Media Marketing.

This offer is limited to the first 100 reviewers, and only for reviewers who have purchased a paid copy of the book. You may be required to show proof of purchase and the birth certificate of your first born child, cat, or goldfish. If you don't have a child, cat, or goldfish, you may be required to prove telepathically that you bought the book.

▶ QUESTIONS AND MORE INFORMATION

I **encourage** my students to ask questions! If you have questions, submit them via https://www.jm-seo.org/contact/. There are two sorts of questions: ones that I know instantly, for which I'll zip you an email answer right away, and ones I do not know instantly, in which case I will investigate and we'll figure out the answer together.

As a teacher, I learn most from my students. So please don't be shy!

▶ COPYRIGHT AND DISCLAIMER

Uh! Legal stuff! Get ready for some fun:

This is a completely **unofficial** guide to Twitter marketing. Twitter has not <u>endorsed this guide</u>, nor has anyone affiliated with Twitter been involved in the production of this guide.

That's a *good thing*. This guide is **independent**. My aim is to "tell it as I see it," giving you no-nonsense information on how to succeed at Twitter marketing.

In addition, please note the following:

- All trademarks are the property of their respective owners. I have no relationship with nor endorsement from the mark holders. Any use of their marks is so I can provide information to you.

- Any reference to or citation of third party products or services whether for Twitter, LinkedIn, Facebook, Yelp, Google / Google+, Yahoo, Bing, Pinterest, YouTube, or other businesses, search engines, or social media platforms, should not be construed as an endorsement of those products or services tools, nor as a warranty as to their effectiveness or compliance with the terms of service with any search engine or social media platform.

The information used in this guide was derived in July, 2015. However, social media marketing changes rapidly, so please be aware that scenarios, facts, and conclusions are subject to change without notice.

Additional Disclaimer. Internet marketing is an art, and not a science. Any changes to your Internet marketing strategy, including SEO, Social Media Marketing, and AdWords, is at your own risk. Neither Jason McDonald, Excerpti Communications, Inc., nor the JM Internet Group assumes any responsibility for the effect of any changes you may, or may not, make to your website or AdWords advertising based on the information in this guide.

» ACKNOWLEDGEMENTS

No man is an island. I would like to thank my beloved wife, Noelle Decambra, for helping me hand-in-hand as the world's best moderator for our online classes, and as my personal cheerleader in the book industry. Gloria McNabb has done her usual tireless job as first assistant, including updating this edition as well the *Social Media Marketing* toolbook. Alex Facklis and Hannah McDonald also assisted with tools and research. I would also like to thank my black Labrador retriever, Buddy, for countless walks and games of fetch, during which I refined my ideas about marketing and about life.

And, again, a huge thank you to my students – online, in San Francisco, and at Stanford Continuing Studies. You challenge me, you inspire me, and you motivate me!

TWITTER

Do you Tweet? Should you? Twitter is among the most misunderstood of all the social media. On the one hand, it dominates news and pop culture, giving Twitter a brand presence second only to Facebook. *Ellen DeGeneres tweets. Barack Obama tweets. CBS News tweets*. And so the logic goes: *you better tweet, too*. But, on the other hand, Twitter is full of noise, news and craziness: it isn't necessarily a good marketing venue for many businesses. In fact, many businesses tweet and no one is really listening, so Twitter is just an effort in futility.

In short, Twitter can be an **effective marketing channel** for your business, or Twitter can be a **huge waste of time**. Which is it? Should you use Twitter, and if so, how? The answer, of course, is "it depends." It depends on whether your customers are on Twitter, and whether you can systematically implement a Twitter marketing strategy.

In this chapter, you'll learn how Twitter works, how to figure out if Twitter is a good opportunity for your business, how to set up your Twitter account, and – most importantly – how to tweet effectively. Throughout, I will point you to free tools and resources for more information as well as worksheets to guide you step-by-step. Even if you are already tweeting, you'll learn how to really use Twitter for marketing as opposed to just wasting your time.

By the end of this chapter, you'll understand how Twitter works, be able to research whether Twitter has potential for your company, and be on your way to implementing a step-by-step Twitter marketing plan. A little bird just called.

Let's get started!

TO DO LIST:

>> EXPLORE HOW TWITTER WORKS

One way to understand **Twitter** is to think of Twitter as a **micro blogging** platform. Blogs are all about having an inspiration for a blog post, composing a strong headline, and writing some detailed paragraphs about the topic. Twitter is very similar, just a lot shorter - 140 characters, to be exact.

Let's compare writing a blog post and composing a tweet.

When you write a blog post, you a) conceptualize a **topic** (*hopefully of interest to your target audience*), b) write a **headline** and the **blog post** itself, and c) **promote** your blog post. Similarly, within the constraints of a 140 character tweet, you a) conceptualize a **topic** of interest to your (potential) followers, b) write a **headline / tweet** (they're basically one-and-the-same on Twitter), and c) **promote** your tweet.

TWITTER IS MICROBLOGGING

One difference apparent right from the start is that on Twitter a tweet often points outwards to an in-depth blog post, a video, an infographic, or an image. A tweet can often be just a "headline" pointing out to the "rest of the story," but many tweets are self-standing as well. But in either case, composing a tweet is very similar to composing a blog post.

Twitter is Like Facebook (and LinkedIn and Pinterest...)

Structurally speaking, Twitter also share many similarities with other social media. Like Facebook, LinkedIn, Pinterest and other social media, your Twitter account (a.k.a., "Page") can be "followed" ("liked") by others, who are alerted in their news feeds when you tweet new items. In addition, tweets can be discovered through *#hashtags* plus people can *retweet* (share) your tweets, respond to them, or favorite them, thereby drawing the attention of their followers to you.

The names may have changed, but the basic structure of Twitter is not unlike that of Facebook:

- Individuals have *accounts* on Twitter ("profiles" on Facebook).
- Companies have *accounts* on Twitter ("pages" on Facebook).
- If an individual *follows* your account on Twittter ("likes" your Page on Facebook), then when that company tweets it will show up in the *news feed* of that individual.
- Individuals can
    - *favorite* a tweet – "like" a post on Facebook;
    - *respond* to a tweet – "comment" on Facebook; and/or
    - *re-tweet* a tweet to their followers (reshare posts on Facebook).

Tweets are short (less than 140 characters), and consist usually of text but can include links, graphics and videos.

The structure of Twitter is quite similar to that of Facebook; the big differences are that Twitter is shorter, faster, and noisier than Facebook.

Let's review the differences in detail.

How Twitter is Unique

First and foremost, Twitter is the most open of all the social media. Anyone can set up a Twitter account in literally minutes, and start tweeting – there's no real authentication. And anyone can listen in: there's no required friending or connecting as on Facebook or LinkedIn. Indeed, even people who do not follow you can easily find and read your tweets. They can even contact you, without your pre-approval. Let me repeat these facts:

anyone can instantly set up a Twitter account and start tweeting: no authentication required;

anyone can listen in to anyone on Twitter: no friending required; and

anyone can talk to **anyone** via Twitter: it's completely open!

Twitter is Open

Twitter is like a massive 24/7 talk radio station, or a water cooler conversation: anyone can talk, and anyone can listen, no authentication required and no requirement that the person talking have any expertise or intelligence on the matter.

> Twitter is as open as talk radio, even more so because not only can anyone listen in, anyone can broadcast!

So anyone can talk on Twitter, but is *anyone really listening*? That's a different question and the answer varies a great deal based on your industry, your status, and your skill at building an audience on Twitter. Also, because Twitter is short and news-oriented as well as open to any sort of broadcasting, it is incredibly noisy and full of silly Internet insanity.

Twitter is Noisy, Really Noisy

Because of its openness and because of its focus on short, newsy content, Twitter is a blizzard of information with lots and lots of noise obfuscating the interesting stuff. Whereas Facebook is all about friends, family, and fun "as if" you are at a company picnic or family reunion, Twitter is "as if" you were listening to all talk radio stations and all cable TV stations at the same time.

Amidst the noise of Twitter, the trick is to focus in on your customers and any marketing opportunities.

Twitter's Culture

For any social media, it's important to understand its culture. Twitter is fast-paced and used primarily to share news (about everything) and/or to share gossip (about pop culture and politics). If, for example, your business lives in an industry that thrives on news, Twitter may be great for you. If, for example, your business is connected to politics, news, or pop culture, Twitter may be essential to your marketing efforts. If your business is about coupons, special deals, and foodie events, Twitter may be an amazing marketing opportunity. If you attend industry trade shows or want to reach specific journalists hungry for story ideas, Twitter can be your secret marketing weapon.

Throughout, keep your eye on how to "tune in" to the appropriate conversations on Twitter and "tune out" the blizzard of useless Twitter noise. Like talk radio or the 365 channels on cable TV, it's all about tuning in to an audience to succeed at Twitter marketing.

Untuned, your Twitter marketing will be a waste of time!

Sign up for Twitter

If you haven't already signed up for Twitter, simply go to http://jmlinks.com/1h. For more complete information on setting up your business, go to http://jmlinks.com/1i.

The basics of a business Twitter account are as follows:

- **Your Account / Your Username / Twitter Handle**. A username such as **@jmgrp** becomes your Twitter handle or URL (http://twitter.com/jmgrp) and shows up in your tweets. Choose a short user name that reflects your brand identity. **Shorter names are better** because tweets are limited to 140 characters and your username or "handle" counts as characters. As with most social media, you need an email address to sign up, or you can use a mobile phone number; unlike Facebook pages, you can only have one email address / password / user – or you can use third party apps like Hootsuite (http://www.hootsuite.com/) or Tweetdeck (http://www.tweetdeck.com/) to let multiple people access your account.
- **Profile Photo**. This is essentially the same as a profile photo on Facebook. The recommend images size is 400x400 pixels. It shows on your Tweets when viewed in a follower's news feed.
- **Bio**. You have 160 characters to explain your company brand, products, and/or services. Be sure to include a http:// URL link to your company website.
- **Header Image**. Similar to the Facebook cover photo, you get 1500x500 pixels to run as a banner across your account page.
- **Pinned Tweet**. You can "pin" a tweet to the top of your Twitter account, so that it shows first when users click up to your Twitter page. For example, compose a tweet that promotes your email newsletter, and then "pin" this to the top of your Twitter account.

Here's a screenshot of how to "pin" a Tweet:

Jason McDonald @jasoneg3 · 1h

Free tools for social media marketing. Social Media Toolbook. Coupon code: social3762 jm-seo.org/?p=1103

Jason McDonald @jasoneg3 · 1

"Is Donald Trump

Scam?" #marketi

jamesaltucher.co

Share via Direct Message

Copy link to Tweet

Embed Tweet

Pin to your profile page

Delete Tweet

ian 4

n...

View

Essentially, find the tweet you want to pin, click on the dot dot dot icon, and then click on "pin to your profile page."

To access any of the other settings and features, go to your page on Twitter (as for example, http://twitter.com/jmgrp), be sure you are logged in, and click on the "edit profile" button in the far right of the screen. Also note that by clicking on your (small) Twitter profile picture at the top right of the screen, you can access your account settings (or go here: https://twitter.com/settings/security when logged in).

Here's a screenshot:

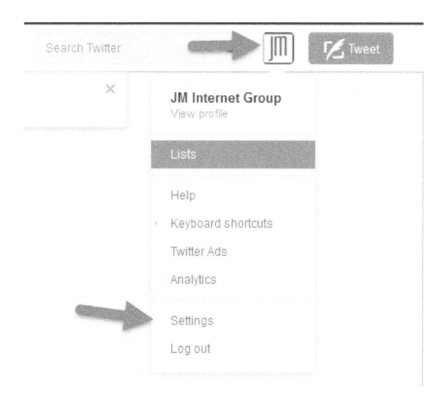

Not much can be customized, but in this day of Internet hacking and piracy, I recommend that you turn on **login verification**, which will require a mobile phone code for any new login.

Following and Followers

Now that you've set up your account, you can "follow" people or brands on Twitter by finding their Twitter accounts and clicking on the "follow" link. Similarly, people can follow you on Twitter by doing the same.

This structure is the same as on Facebook: when people follow you on Twitter, they see your tweets in their news feed subject to the clutter of the rapidly-moving Twitter news feed and a secret algorithm in Twitter that attempts to prioritize interactive Tweets (e.g., similar to Facebook *Edgerank*). Similarly, you can share the tweets of others (called *retweeting* or *RT*) to your own followers and others can share your tweets to their followers. It's *social* media after all.

Understand a Tweet

Tweets are the heart and soul of Twitter, and correspond to posts on Facebook. A tweet is limited to 140 characters, and as you type your tweet into your Twitter account it will give you a convenient countdown of the remaining characters. If you use an app like

Hootsuite, that app will also give you a character count. Or you can use a service like http://www.lettercount.com/ and pre-count your characters.

Think of a tweet as a news headline or very short micro blog post with just a little supporting information. If you tweet a link to a blog post or other Web page, use a URL shortener like http://bit.ly.com, http://tinyurl.com/, or the "shortlink" feature in WordPress, so as not to waste characters. To read Twitter's own description of how to tweet visit http://jmlinks.com/1j. You can create a self-standing tweet, or you can tweet "outlinks" to blog posts, videos, or images.

Here's a screenshot of a tweet:

Notice that if your tweet references an external URL, and that URL has a featured image, Twitter will display that image in this case a photo of the book cover.

Understand Hashtags

A hashtag (#) in a tweet indicates a keyword or theme and is clickable in a tweet. Think of a hashtag as a keyword / subject / theme about which people are talking: *sports, the Oakland A's, global warming, the 2016 presidential campaign, the Academy awards.* Hashtags should be short, and can NOT include spaces. Anyone can create one, and the success, or failure, of a hashtag is a function of whether many, or just a few, people use them. And, yes because Twitter is totally open there is no control: anyone can use them for any purpose, and a hashtag can overlap two discussions.

Anyone can create a hashtag! Anyone can chime in on a hashtag! No one controls a hashtag!

How it's used, however, is a function of the crowd: the crowd decides what the hashtag really means.

To find existing hashtags, use http://hashtagify.me or simply search Twitter using the # hashtag in front of a topic such as *#organicfood* or *#free*. Note that hashtags can NOT include spaces. So it's *#organicfood* not *#organic food*. Or just search Twitter by keyword and look for the # hashtag symbol. For example, here's a screenshot of a tweet with the hashtags highlighted in yellow:

Green Breeze Imports @GreenBreezeImpt · Jul 11
#Organic #Natural #Body #Lotion. Check it out! Keep #skin #smooth and #soft. amazon.com/dp/B010RFVQRI

I recommend that you research, identify, and maintain a running list of *hashtags* that are important to your company.

#HASHTAGS DESIGNATE CONVERSATIONS ON TWITTER

In the tweet above, the hashtags *#organic* and *#natural* are "themes" around which people converse on Twitter. By including hashtags in your Tweets, you can be found by non-followers who are interested in, and following, that topic on Twitter. For example, if you are a seller of organic baby food and have a new flavor out, you might tweet with hashtags as follows:

Hey followers! Our super baby plum recipe is out. **#babyfood #organic #natural #food**. http://bit.ly/1234

These hashtags become clickable in a tweet, and for people who are interested in that topic, your tweet becomes part of an enormous conversation around that theme. So, finding popular, relevant hashtags and tweeting on them is a good promotion strategy on Twitter. Remember, however, that you have to stand out and get attention amidst all the noise!

Understand the @ Sign or Handle

The @ sign designates a Twitter account, often called a "handle" on Twitter. When included in a tweet, it does two things:

- It becomes **clickable**. Anyone who sees this tweet can click on the @handle and go up to that account to view the account and possibly follow that person on Twitter; and
- It **shows up in the news feed of that person** and **sends an email alert** to him or her that they have been mentioned. This is called a *mention*. A *mention* means essentially that: someone has mentioned you (your Twitter account) in a Tweet.

Here's a screenshot:

KQED (@KQED) has tweeted to its followers that Barry Manilow (@barrymanilow) will be on its show July 4th, PBS. Anyone seeing this tweet can click "up" to Barry Manilow's account, and Barry Manilow would have received a "mention" notification in his account news feed.

USING THE @ SIGN, YOU CAN TWEET TO ANYONE

Importantly, this openness means that you can tweet "to" anyone on Twitter: it's completely open, and – unlike Facebook or LinkedIn – you do not need "pre-approval" to converse with someone via Twitter (more about this later, when we discuss promoting your Twitter account).

Again, when your Tweet contains the @handle of someone else, that generates an alert in their news feed and often via email. **Via Twitter, you can tweet to anyone**!

Understand Mentions and Retweets

We've already explained a **mention**. When someone includes your @handle in their Tweet, that's called a mention: clickable by anyone following them, to go "up" to your account and learn about you or your business.

A **retweet** is a special type of mention. In it, person *A* retweets the tweet of person *B*. Meaning, he takes your tweet and tweets it out to his followers. Imagine if Ellen DeGeneres recapped your joke on her TV show. That "retweet" of your joke would spur her followers to learn about you, and might result in a massive increase in your follower count.

Here's a screenshot:

Ellen DeGeneres ✓
@TheEllenShow

Yeah I did. RT @justinbieber: I think today was our best hang out yet. @TheEllenShow u got me. Lol

Ellen is "retweeting" Justin Bieber's tweet about how great their interaction was on her TV show. In this way, her fans see Justin Bieber's Twitter account @justinbieber and can learn about him, and possibly follow him, thereby increasing his follower count. Ellen and Justin are essentially having a public conversation via Twitter.

You don't have to be a Hollywood star to do this: identify important people in your industry and converse with them via the @sign (handles). Your followers can see this conversation, and their followers can see it too (if the person responds to you) – thereby cross-pollinating your accounts. (See technical details below).

Here's some esoterica about mentions or retweets. When you tweet directly at someone (by including their account (@sign) in your tweet), that tweet is visible to only those folks who follow both accounts. If you put a dot "." before the @ sign, your tweet shows up in the news feed (officially called your "timeline" on Twitter, but not to be confused with the "timeline" of Facebook) of all of your followers, even if they do not follow the menteiond account. For example, if I tweet:

@katyperry love your music, give me free concert tickets!

> (shows to ONLY those people who follow @jasoneg3 AND @katyperry) and it shows in Katy Perry's own timeline (if she actually checks it)).

vs.

.@katyperry loved your concert, give me free concert tickets!

(shows to ALL people who follow @jasoneg3 AND it shows in Katy Perry's own timeline (if she actually checks it)).

To read more about the "dot" in front of the "@" sign in more detail, visit http://jmlinks.com/2k. For the official Twitter guide to Twitter for Business, visit https://business.twitter.com/ and for the official Twitter help files, visit https://support.twitter.com/.

▶▶ MAKE AN INVENTORY OF LIKES & DISLIKES ON TWITTER

Now that you understand the basics of how Twitter works, it's time to research whether your customers are on Twitter and identify competitors in your industry who are on Twitter and/or successful businesses on Twitter to make an inventory of your likes and dislikes.

Find Accounts on Twitter

Stay signed into your Twitter account. There are several ways to find accounts to follow on Twitter:

- **Visit their Websites**. Most big brands will have a prominent link to Twitter, right on their Website. For example, go to http://www.rei.com/ or http://www.wholefoods.com/, find the Twitter link, click on it, and hit follow. Go to your competitor websites and do the same.
- **Search on Twitter**. While logged in to your account, go to the top right of the screen and in the "Search Twitter" box, enter the names of competitors, businesses you like, or keywords. To find stuff on Twitter about organic food, just type in "organic food" into the search box. Then, when you find an account you like, just click "follow" and you are now following it.
- **Advanced Search on Twitter**. You can find Twitter Advanced Search by first doing a search, then in the results

Here's a screenshot:

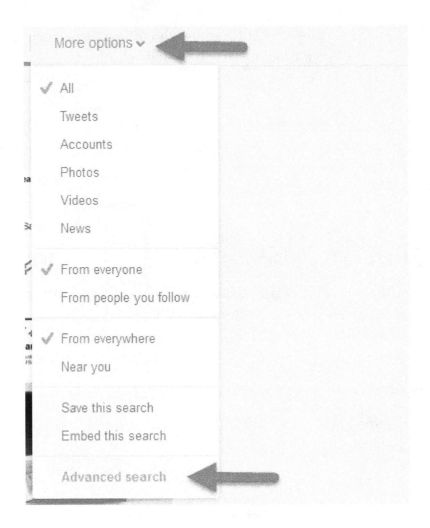

You can also just visit this link: https://twitter.com/search-advanced.

Outside of Twitter, go to Google and type in *site:twitter.com* and your keywords. For example, on Google, *site:twitter.com "organic food"* will identify Twitter accounts with that keyword. Google is often a better way to find Twitter *accounts*, whereas Twitter search is a better way to browse individual *tweets*. Remember: there is no space between site: and twitter – it's *site:twitter.com* not *site: twitter.com*. To see this in action, go to http://jmlinks.com/2j.

Another great place to identify interesting companies is WEFOLLOW (http://wefollow.com/). Type in your keywords, and this site identifies the most powerful accounts on Twitter.

Once you follow companies, you can browse their Twitter pages easily by clicking on the "following" link at the top left of the page while you are logged in to your Twitter account. Here's a screenshot –

Note that Twitter is completely open: anyone can see who you follow via your public Twitter account (unlike on, say, Facebook, where only you know whom you are following).

Your todo here is to identify companies on Twitter, both in and outside of your industry, so that you can inventory what you like and dislike. Here are some inventory questions:

- **Username**. Usernames should be short yet convey the brand. Do you like / dislike the usernames of brands that you see?
- **Profile Picture**. As is true in all social media, the profile pictures shows when viewed on someone else's timeline. Do you like / dislike the profile pictures of various companies on Twitter? Why or why not?
- **Header Photo**. Similarly to the Facebook cover photo, this wide banner dominates that account visuals. How are competitors and other businesses using the header photo on Twitter?
- **Pinned Tweets**. Are any brands using the pinned tweet feature? If so, how?
- **Account Bio**. How are brands using their bio to market via Twitter? Do you see any opportunities or pitfalls here?

Posting or Tweeting Strategy

You'll quickly realize that Twitter offers little customization, and that most of the action on Twitter has to do with *posting strategy* or what would precisely be called *tweeting strategy*. What are businesses tweeting, and why? What is their *posting rhythm*? Similar to all social media, the idea is to spur interactivity, get shares (retweets), and drive traffic to desired actions.

Pay attention to companies in your industry as well as hashtags (see below) in your industry, all the while asking the question: are our customers on Twitter? If so, what are they tweeting about?

Let's review some accounts on Twitter and reverse-engineer their posting strategies. Do the same for businesses that you like and/or competitors in your industry.

Twitter Marketing: Common Uses

Here are common uses of Twitter and example accounts:

- **Celebrities**. Examples are Katy Perry (https://twitter.com/katyperry) , Justin Bieber (https://twitter.com/justinbieber), Ellen Degeneres (https://twitter.com/TheEllenShow).
    - ○ **Marketing Goals**: stay top of mind, get social shares, use Twitter to cross-promote their concerts and TV shows, **posting rhythm** of *fun, fun, fun, fun, buy my concert tickets* etc.
- **Politicians**. Examples are Hillary Clinton (https://twitter.com/hillaryclinton), Barack Obama (https://twitter.com/potus), Bill de Blasio (https://twitter.com/billdeblasio).
    - ○ **Marketing Goals**: stay top of mind, get social shares, use Twitter to motivate followers to take political action. **Posting rhythm** of newsworthy, newsworthy, newsworthy, take political action or donate...
- **Political Causes and Non-Profits.** Examples are Greenpeace (https://twitter.com/greenpeace), Red Cross (https://twitter.com/redcross), Catholic Charities (https://twitter.com/ccharitiesusa).
    - ○ **Marketing Goals:** stay top of mind, get social shares, use Twitter followers to take political action or make donations. Posting rhythm is similar to politicians.
- **Brands.** Examples are REI (https://twitter.com/rei), Gucci (https://twitter.com/gucci), Marth Stewart Living (https://twitter.com/MS_Living).
    - ○ **Marketing Goals:** stay top of mind, get social shares, use Twitter followers to connect to buy actions, also use Twitter as an "insider" or "best customer" channel for secret coupons, inside deals and information. **Posting rhythm** is fun, fun, fun, fun, buy my stuff.

- **Restaurants and Food Trucks.** Examples are Kogi BBQ
  (https://twitter.com/kogibbq), Ricky's Fish Tacos
  (https://twitter.com/rickysfishtacos), Newark Natural Foods
  (https://twitter.com/newarkfoods).
  - o **Marketing Goals**. stay top of mind, get social shares, use Twitter to drive
    real-world traffic to a store or restaurant, usually looking for insider
    information or special deals / coupons.

For most for-profit businesses, common marketing goals for Twitter are:

- **Stay top of mind / one touch to many**. To the extent that your users are on
  Twitter (usually to follow up-to-the-minute news), you can use Twitter to
  continually remind users about your company, product, and/or service.
- **Insider / loyalty programs**. If you are a brand with a core group of loyal
  customers (e.g., REI's loyal group of outdoor fanatics, or Gucci's loyal group of
  fashion addicts), you can use Twitter to stay in touch with this elite group and
  reward them with insider information, tips, special deals, and even coupons.
- **Coupons / bargains**. If you use coupons or discounts, especially in retail,
  customers commonly scan Twitter for coupons and special deals.
- **Foodies / coupons / bargains / what's cookin'**. Especially in the food truck
  industry, but in any big downtown area with a lunch scene, foodies look to
  Twitter to identify special deals, coupons, and what's cookin'.
- **On-going Discussions**. By using #hashtags (e.g., #AIDS, #globalwarming,
  #obamacare), you can participate in an on-going global discussion and thereby
  market your products. A special case of this is trade shows, which often use a
  hashtag (#CES for Consumer Electronics Show, for example) to allow
  participants to converse via Twitter.
- **News Alerts**. To the extent that you generate and/or participate in news,
  Twitter is the go-to service for breaking news (especially vis hashtags and
  trending searches).
- **Political Action**. For non-profits and political groups, Twitter is the go-to place
  to organize politically and discuss politics.

Identify companies who do Twitter well, and reverse engineer them

For your first TODO, download the **Twitter Research Worksheet**. For the worksheet, go to https://www.jm-seo.org/workbooks (click on Twitter, enter the code 'twitter2016' to register if you have not already done so), and click on the link to the "Twitter Research Worksheet." You'll answer questions as to whether your potential customers are on Twitter, identify brands to follow, and inventory what you like and dislike about their Twitter set up and marketing strategy.

≫ BRAINSTORM AND EXECUTE A TWEETING STRATEGY

Optimizing your account on Twitter is pretty straightforward. As indicated above, a good way to do this is to compare / contrast pages that you like and use your inventory list to identify ToDos. So, comparing Taco Bell (https://twitter.com/tacobell), the White House (https://twitter.com/whlive), and Kogi BBQ (https://twitter.com/kogibbq), let's go down the short list. As indicated above, the main elements are:

- **Your Account / Your Username / Twitter Handle**. A username such as **@jmgrp** becomes your Twitter URL (http://twitter.com/jmgrp) and shows up in your tweets. Choose a short user name that reflects your brand identity. **Shorter names are better** because tweets are limited to 140 characters and your username or "handle" counts as characters. As with most social media, you need an email address to sign up, or you can use a mobile phone number; unlike Facebook pages, you can only have one email address / password / user – or you can use third party apps like Hootsuite to control your account.
- **Profile Photo**. This is essentially the same as a profile photo on Facebook. The recommend images size is 400x400 pixels. It shows on your Tweets when viewed in a follower's news feed.
- **Bio**. You have 160 characters to explain your company brand, products, and/or services. Be sure to include a URL link to your company website.
- **Header Image**. Similar to the Facebook cover photo, you get 1500x500 pixels to run as a banner across your account page.
- **Pinned Tweet**. You can "pin" a tweet to the top of the page, so that it shows first when users click up to your Twitter account page. For example, compose a tweet

that promotes your email newsletter, and then "pin" this to the top of your Twitter account.

If you haven't already signed up for Twitter, simply go to http://jmlinks.com/1h. For more complete information on setting up your business, go to http://jmlinks.com/1i.

That's all there is to Twitter at a structural level. The real work begins in identifying a tweeting strategy. What will you tweet? Who will care? Let's reverse engineer some companies and their tweeting strategies:

Kogi BBQ (https://twitter.com/kogibbq). Their tweeting strategy is 90% about the location of the taco truck, with a few tweets about "what's cooking" or "insider specials," and the occasional back-and-forth with a hard-core Kogi fan about the joys of Korean BBQ. That's it.

REI (https://twitter.com/rei). Their tweets are largely off-loads to blog posts, YouTube videos, and Instagram photos about the fun of outdoor activities, some participatory contests for hard-core REI fans, headline links to in-depth blog posts on outdoor fun, and about 10% shameless "buy our stuff isn't this a cool product" tweets. Like many retailers, REI uses Twitter as a place to communicate deals, insider information, and special offers to its most devoted customers.

Woot (https://twitter.com/woot). Their tweets are 100% about discounts and bargains, as Woot (owned now by Amazon) is all about discounts and special deals. It's the home shopping network gone Twitter.

Greenpeace (https://twitter.com/greenpeace). This non-profit tweets photos that inspire about wildlife and nature, links to blog posts about environmental issues, and political calls to action.

Cato Institute (https://twitter.com/catoinstitute). This political action organization tweets about politics from a conservative perspective, with offlinks to its blog and videos plus the occasional call to action.

Zak George (https://twitter.com/zakgeorge). A dog trainer and huge YouTube success, Zak George tweets links to his YouTube videos, some links to his Facebook page, and the occasional tweet about a sponsored product.

Your job is to reverse engineer competitors or companies you admire in terms of their tweeting strategy. What are they tweeting (blog posts, pictures, infographics, videos), and why are they tweeting it (to stay top of mind, sell stuff, get viewers on YouTube). Who is following them and why? What's in it for the followers? How does all this tweeting activity lead ultimately to some sort of sale or business action?

For your second TODO, download the **Twitter Tweeting Strategy Worksheet**. For the worksheet, go to https://www.jm-seo.org/workbooks (click on Twitter, enter the code 'twitter2016' to register if you have not already done so), and click on the link to the "Twitter Tweeting Strategy Worksheet." You'll answer questions to help you understand what other companies are doing on Twitter, and begin to outline your own tweeting strategy.

Content is King

As you work on a tweeting strategy, you'll quickly realize you need a lot of content! Remember: create a content marketing system of:

- **Other people's content**. Relevant content in your industry. By curating out the garbage and identify the cool, fun, interesting stuff, you can use other people's content to help your tweets stay top of mind.
- **Your own content**. Twitter is all about off-loads to blog posts, infographics, images, photos, videos, Memes, and other types of your own content. Twitter and blogging go together like peas and carrots, while Twitter and video go together like scotch and soda.

To identify relevant content from other people, I recommend setting up a Feedly account (http://www.feedly.com/) and using tools like Topsy (http://www.topsy.com/), Buzzsumo (http://www.buzzsumo.com), and Google Alerts (https://www.google.com/alerts). Organize these tools into topic groups, and then as you find content useful to your target audience, "tweet out" that content. Use a tool like Hootsuite (http://www.hootsuite.com/) to schedule your tweets in advance.

As for your own content, Twitter is best used by staying on topic and sharing original useful content such as in-depth blog posts, free eBooks or webinars, infographics and instructographics, videos on YouTube. Twitter is a headline service pointing to the "rest of the story" on your blog, video, or infographic.

» PROMOTE YOUR TWITTER ACCOUNT AND TWEETS

Once you've set up your Twitter account, and begun to populate it with tweets on a regular basis, you've essentially "set up" your party on Twitter. Now it's time to send out the invitations.

In and of itself, a Twitter Page will not be self-promoting! You've got to promote it!

Assuming your Twitter account shares lots of yummy, useful, fun, provocative content that when seen by a user will entice him or her to "follow" you on Twitter, here are some common ways to promote your Twitter account and Tweets:

- **Real World to Social.** Don't forget the real world! If you are a museum store, for example, be sure that the cashiers recommend to people that they "follow" you on Twitter? *Why? Because they'll get insider tips, fun do-it-yourself posts, announcements on upcoming museum and museum store events, etc.* Get your staff to promote Twitter in that important face-to-face interaction. If you're a barbeque truck in Los Angeles, post signs to "follow us on Twitter" on the trucks, and have staff cajole customers to "follow you." *Why follow you on Twitter? To learn where the taco truck is, to get special deals, and to learn what's cooking.* Use the real world to promote your Twitter account, and be ready to explain "why" they should follow you on Twitter. What's in it for them?
- **Cross-Promotion**. Link your website to your Twitter Page, your blog posts to your Twitter Page, your YouTube to your Twitter Page, etc. Notice how big brands like REI do this: one digital property promotes another digital property.
- **Email**. Email your customer list and ask them to follow you on Twitter. Again, you must explain what's in it for them.
- **Twitter Internal**. Interact with other accounts via the @ sign, share their content, comment on timely topics using #hashtags, and reach out to complementary pages to work with you on co-promotion. (See below).
- **Use Twitter Plugins**. Twitter has numerous plugins that allow you to "embed" your Twitter Page on your website, and thereby nurture cross promotion. To learn more about plugins, visit https://dev.twitter.com/web/overview. Among the better ones –
  - **The Tweet Button**. Make it easy for people to tweet your content (e.g., blog posts).
  - **The Follow Button**. Make it easy for Web visitors to follow you on Twitter.

- **Leverage your Fans**. People who like your Twitter Page are your best promoters. Do everything you can to get them to retweet you to their own followers. Remember, it's *social* (!) media, and encouraging your customers to share your content is the name of the game. You want to leverage your fans as much as possible to share your content.

DON'T FORGET THE REAL WORLD AS A TWITTER PROMOTION STRATEGY

Three Special Ways to Promote via Twitter.

Twitter has three very special ways to promote yourself or your company that are much stronger than on other social media.

The first is the **hashtag**. Because Twitter is all about news, the use of hashtags (designated on Twitter by the "#" or "hash" sign) on trending or controversial topics is bigger on Twitter than on any other social media. Identify trending or important hashtags and include them in your tweets. Use http://hashtagify.me to identify hashtags in your industry, and don't forget about major trade shows which often have (and promote) their own hashtags. Then include these hashtags in your tweets, and make sure that your tweets are not only on topic but also offlink to something useful, provocative or important. In that way, they'll discover you via a hashtag and then follow you permanently.

Industry Trade Shows and Hashtags

Here's a hashtag use you do not want to miss: industry trade shows. Nearly every industry has THE trade show, or a few KEY trade shows. Nowadays, these will have hashtags, such as *#CES2014* for the 2014 Consumer Electronics Show. Pre-identify the hashtags of your own industry trade show(s) as well as subordinate, session or topic hashtags, and start tweeting on those theme before, during and shortly after the show. Attendees know to look for the show hashtags to find out what's cool, exciting, and worth visiting.

For many businesses, simply knowing the hashtag of "the" industry conference and tweeting during the yearly, or twice yearly, trade conference in and of itself will justify using Twitter for marketing:

> *Hey #CES2014 attendees! Come by out booth by 2:30 pm for a free laser wand give-away.*

Identify the Twitter account of the industry trade show(s), and they'll easily show you the relevant hashtags. Make sure you have a robust Twitter account set up before the big show, and then during the show start tweeting on show-related hashtags. For many businesses, the trade show use of Twitter is the most important marketing use of Twitter.

The second promotion strategy is what I call **@someonefamous**. The idea here is to reach out and "have a conversation" with someone more famous (with more followers) than you. Think of it like Dr. Phil making it on the Oprah Winfrey show: her audience saw this new "doctor," and some of her fans became his fans. The trick is to find business partners, complementary companies, or other people / companies on Twitter who are influencers and who have more and/or different fan bases than you.

One tool to do this is to use WeFollow (http://www.wefollow.com/) to identify the most influential people on Twitter. Other useful tools to use are Buzzsumo (http://www.buzzsumo.com/) or Topsy (http://www.topsy.com/). Search for your keywords and identify influencers tweeting about those topics. Identifying them is the easy part. The hard part is getting them to engage in a Twitter conversation with you. You have to convince them to have a conversation with you on Twitter, and then once you're talking to their fans... convince their fans to follow you, too.

Once you are lucky enough to start a conversation with someone more famous than you, remember to use the "dot" in front of the "@" sign to correctly broadcast your message. To learn more about this, visit http://jmlinks.com/2k.

Pitch Journalists via Twitter

Here's a key use of twitter you do not want to miss: pitching journalists via Twitter about your company, products, or services as "story ideas:"

- **@journalists**. Identify journalists on Twitter, find their handles, and tweet "to" the journalists, pitching them on story ideas. Journalists love Twitter because it's where stories break first. They listen to their Twitter feeds as businesses, organizations, and individuals "pitch" them on story ideas via Twitter.

Indeed, you can even advertise to select lists of journalists by using username targeting on Twitter (see below).

The third Twitter promotion strategy is the **retweet**. By posting items that are funny, scandalous, interesting, shocking, outrageous or otherwise highly contagious, you get people to retweet your tweets, thereby (again) allowing their followers to see you, and hopefully begin to follow you as well. To research what is retweeted in your industry, simply do a Twitter search with the words RT in front of your keywords. For an example, visit http://jmlinks.com/2l.

Advertise

Besides these three promotion methods, there's (gasp!) paid advertising on Twitter. You can promote your tweets as well as create custom advertising campaigns to promote your account and/or clicks to your website. To learn more about advertising on Twitter visit https://biz.twitter.com/start-advertising or https://ads.twitter.com/. Because journalists and bloggers often follow Twitter intensely for breaking news, one strategy is to make an "influencer list" on influencers on Twitter, and then advertise your tweets directly to those high-impact Twitterers. To learn more about username targeting on Twitter, visit http://jmlinks.com/1k.

» MEASURE YOUR RESULTS

Measuring the success or failure of your Twitter marketing can be a challenge. Let's look at it from the "bottom up" in terms of items a marketer might want to know or measure vis-a-vis Twitter:

- **Sales or Sales Leads**. Have tweets or Twitter marketing resulted in actual sales leaders (completed feedback forms for a free offer, consultation, eBook, download, etc.) and/or eCommerce sales?
- **Branding / Awareness**. Has Twitter increased our brand awareness and/or improved our brand image?
- **Top of Mind / One Touch to Many**. Has Twitter helped us to stay "top of mind," by reminding potential customers of our company, products, and/or services?

- **Tweet Interactivity**. Have people read our tweets? Interactive with our tweets by favoriting them, and/or retweeted our tweets?
- **Twitter Account**. Is our follower count increasing, and if so, by how much and how fast? Where are our followers physically located, and what are their demographic characteristics?

The last of these is the easiest to measure: simply record your Twitter follower count each month, and keep a record of it month-to-month. I generally do this on my *Keyword Worksheet*, where I also track inbound links to my website, and my review count on review media such as Google+ and Yelp. (Watch a video on a Keyword Worksheet at http://jmlinks.com/1l).

Analytics Inside of Twitter

Inside of Twitter, click on your profile picture on the top right of the screen, and then in the pull-down menu, click on Analytics. Here's a screenshot:

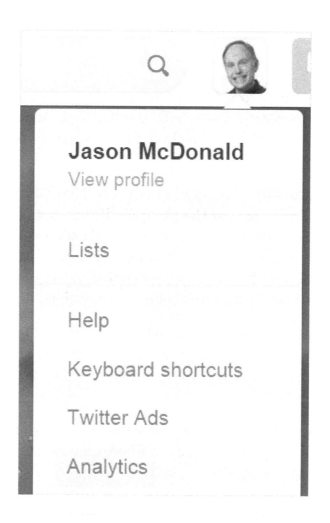

There you can see which tweets gained the most impressions, as well as engagements by Tweet such as clicks, follows, and retweets. Twitter will also tell you whether links you are sharing are getting clicked on and so on and so forth. Twitter also has a feature called **Twitter cards** that bridges your website to/from Twitter activity According To Twitter:

> With Twitter Cards, you can attach rich photos, videos and media experience to Tweets that drive traffic to your website. Simply add a few lines of HTML to your webpage, and users who Tweet links to your content will have a "Card" added to the Tweet that's visible to all of their followers. (https://dev.twitter.com/cards/overview, browsed 7/8/2015).

If you enabled Twitter cards on your Website, you get attribution for your Web content plus more data on that inside of Twitter. Learn more at https://dev.twitter.com/cards/overview.

Google Analytics

Most of us want to drive traffic from Twitter to our website, or even better to our ecommerce store or to download a free eBook or software package to get a sales lead. Google Analytics will measure how traffic flows from Twitter to your website, and then what happens upon arrival.

Sign up for Google Analytics (https://www.google.com/analytics) and install the required tracking code. Inside of your Google Analytics account on the left column, drill down by clicking on Acquisition > Social > Overview. Then on the right hand side of the screen you'll see a list of Social Networks. Find Twitter on that list, and click on that. Google Analytics will tell you what URLs people clicked to from Twitter to your Website, giving you insights into what types of web content people find attractive.

You can also create a custom Advanced Segment to look at only Twitter traffic and its behavior. For information on how to create custom Advanced Segments in Google Analytics, go to http://jmlinks.com/1f. For the Google help files on Advanced Segments go to http://jmlinks.com/1g.

In sum, inside of Twitter you can see how people interact with your Twitter account and tweets. Inside of Google Analytics, you can see where they land on your website and what they do after they arrive.

⟫ Deliverable: A Twitter Marketing Plan

Now that we've come to the end our chapter on Twitter, your DELIVERABLE has arrived. Go to https://www.jm-seo.org/workbooks (click on Twitter, enter the code 'twitter2016' to register if you have not already done so), and click on the link to the "Twitter Marketing Plan." By filling out this plan, you and your team will establish a vision of what you want to achieve via Twitter.

⟫ Appendix: Top Ten Twitter Marketing Tools and Resources

Here are the top ten tools and resources to help you with Twitter marketing. For an up-to-date list, go to https://www.jm-seo.org/workbooks (click on Twitter, enter the code 'twitter2016' to register if you have not already done so). Click on the *Social Media Toolbook* link, and drill down to the Twitter chapter.

HASHTAGIFY.ME - http://hashtagify.me

> Hashtagify.me allows you to search tens of millions of Twitter hashtags and quickly find the best ones for your needs based on popularity, relationships, languages, influencers and other metrics. Also useful for SEO link building and keyword discovery.
>
> **Rating:** 5 Stars | **Category:** tool

WEFOLLOW.COM - http://wefollow.com

> Another service to identify top Tweeters with the most followers, and to identify popular hashtags. Use this service to identify, by keywords, important influencers in your industry. Then influence the influencers!
>
> **Rating:** 5 Stars | **Category:** service

TWEETDECK - https://tweetdeck.twitter.com

> TweetDeck is your personal browser for staying in touch with what's happening now, connecting you with your contacts across Twitter, Facebook, MySpace, LinkedIn and more. Developed independently, now owned by Twitter.

Rating: 4 Stars | **Category:** service

KEYHOLE - http://keyhole.co

This tool provides real-time social conversation tracking for Twitter, Facebook, and Instagram. Use this tool to measure conversations around your business, identify prospective clients and influencers talking about your services, and find relevant content. Enables tracking of hashtags, keywords, and URLs.

Rating: 4 Stars | **Category:** tool

TAGDEF - https://tagdef.com

Looking to understand what a particular hashtag means? Use this nifty tool to define a hashtag and to research hashtags BEFORE you create or use them.

Rating: 4 Stars | **Category:** tool

TWITALYZER - http://twitalyzer.com

An attempt at making Twitter easier to monitor. Input your Twitter handle (@jmgrp for example) and analyze how influential you are. Or, input a competitor's Twitter handle and do some reverse-engineering.

Rating: 4 Stars | **Category:** service

TWITONOMY - http://twitonomy.com

Twitonomy is a free online Twitter analytics tool which provides a wealth of information about all aspects of Twitter, including in-depth stats on any Twitter user, insights on your followers, mentions, favorites & retweets, and analytics on hashtags. It also lets you monitor tweets, manage your lists, download tweets & reports, and much more. Definitely worth checking out if Twitter is part of your social media strategy.

Rating: 4 Stars | **Category:** tool

FOLLOWERWONK - http://followerwonk.com

Followerwonk helps you explore and grow your social graph. Dig deeper into Twitter analytics: Who are your followers? Where are they located? When do they tweet? Find and connect with new influencers in your niche. Use actionable visualizations to compare your social graph to others. Easily share your reports with the world. Brought to you by Moz.

Rating: 4 Stars | **Category:** tool

HASHTAGS.ORG - http://hashtags.org

Tool which attempts to organize the world's hashtags. Provides hashtag analytics for your brand, business, product, service, event or blog. Input words that matter to you, and Hashtags looks to see the trends on Twitter.

Rating: 4 Stars | **Category:** engine

TWITAHOLIC - http://twitaholic.com

Tracks the most popular Twitter users based on followers. Use this to find top tweeters - sort of a top 100, 200, 300, etc list for the Twitterdom. Also just a great way to find out who's really famous on Twitter. Katy Perry, anyone?

Rating: 4 Stars | **Category:** service

3

TWITTER TOOLS

Twitter is the most open of all the social media platforms. Consequently, it has a cornucopia of free resources and free tools to make your life easier. Below I produce my favorite tools and resources (in rank order). Remember that by registering your copy of the workbook, you can access the Social Media Toolbook, which has all the tools in convenient, clickable PDF format. To register, go to https://www.jm-seo.org/workbooks (click on Twitter, enter the code 'twitter2016' to register if you have not already done so), and click on the link to the *Social Media Toolbook*.

Here are free Twitter tools and resources, sorted with the best items first.

HASHTAGIFY.ME - http://hashtagify.me

> Hashtagify.me allows you to search tens of millions of Twitter hashtags and quickly find the best ones for your needs based on popularity, relationships, languages, influencers and other metrics. Also useful for SEO link building and keyword discovery.

> **Rating:** 5 Stars | **Category:** tool

TOPSY - http://topsy.com

> Real-time Twitter search engine. You can also search the web and videos. VERY important: you can input a URL, e.g., jm-seo.org or chipestimate.com, and see how frequently that URL and its sub URLs have been tweeted. Great way to see your social shares as well as discover what's trending on the blogosphere for more effective blogging.

Rating: 5 Stars | **Category:** engine

TWITTER ADVANCED SEARCH - https://twitter.com/search-advanced

Search to see what others are saying about topics relevant and your organization's interests, before, during, after you use Twitter. Here's a nifty trick: Use the 'Near this place' field to find people in a city near you tweeting on a topic like 'pizza.' Great for local brands.

Rating: 5 Stars | **Category:** tool

WEFOLLOW.COM - http://wefollow.com

Another service to identify top Tweeters with the most followers, and to identify popular hashtags. Use this service to identify, by keywords, important influencers in your industry. Then influence the influencers!

Rating: 5 Stars | **Category:** service

BUZZSUMO - http://buzzsumo.com

Buzzsumo is a 'buzz' monitoring tool for social media. Input a website (domain) and/or a topic and see what people are sharing across Facebook, Twitter, Google+ and other social media. Great for link-building (because what people link to is what they share), and also for social media.

Rating: 5 Stars | **Category:** tool

SOCIALOOMPH - http://socialoomph.com

SocialOomph is a powerful free (and paid) suite of tools to manage and schedule your Twitter and Facebook posts. Imagine going to the beach, forgetting about the office, yet having 67 different Tweets auto-posted...that's what SocialOomph is about. Use technology to appear busy and Facebooking / Tweeting all the time.

Rating: 4 Stars | **Category:** tool

SMALL BUSINESS GUIDE TO TWITTER - http://simplybusiness.co.uk/microsites/twitter-for-small-businesses

> Interactive step-by-step flowchart to using Twitter for small business. Comprised of key questions and linked resources with more information. Covers everything from very basic to advanced topics.
>
> **Rating:** 4 Stars | **Category:** resource

TWEETDECK - https://tweetdeck.twitter.com

> TweetDeck is your personal browser for staying in touch with what's happening now, connecting you with your contacts across Twitter, Facebook, MySpace, LinkedIn and more. Developed independently, now owned by Twitter.
>
> **Rating:** 4 Stars | **Category:** service

MASHABLE TWITTER GUIDE BOOK - http://mashable.com/guidebook/twitter

> Mashable is the No. 1 blog on social media and this is a great introduction to / informational resource for Twitter, and includes how-tos, tips, and instructions from their 'experts'. Enjoy!
>
> **Rating:** 4 Stars | **Category:** overview

KEYHOLE - http://keyhole.co

> This tool provides real-time social conversation tracking for Twitter, Facebook, and Instagram. Use this tool to measure conversations around your business, identify prospective clients and influencers talking about your services, and find relevant content. Enables tracking of hashtags, keywords, and URLs.
>
> **Rating:** 4 Stars | **Category:** tool

TAGDEF - https://tagdef.com

> Looking to understand what a particular hashtag means? Use this nifty tool to define a hashtag and to research hashtags BEFORE you create or use them.

Rating: 4 Stars | **Category:** tool

TWITALYZER - http://twitalyzer.com

An attempt at making Twitter easier to monitor. Input your Twitter handle (@jmgrp for example) and analyze how influential you are. Or, input a competitor's Twitter handle and do some reverse-engineering.

Rating: 4 Stars | **Category:** service

TWITONOMY - http://twitonomy.com

Twitonomy is a free online Twitter analytics tool which provides a wealth of information about all aspects of Twitter, including in-depth stats on any Twitter user, insights on your followers, mentions, favorites & retweets, and analytics on hashtags. It also lets you monitor tweets, manage your lists, download tweets & reports, and much more. Definitely worth checking out if Twitter is part of your social media strategy.

Rating: 4 Stars | **Category:** tool

FOLLOWERWONK - http://followerwonk.com

Followerwonk helps you explore and grow your social graph. Dig deeper into Twitter analytics: Who are your followers? Where are they located? When do they tweet? Find and connect with new influencers in your niche. Use actionable visualizations to compare your social graph to others. Easily share your reports with the world. Brought to you by Moz.

Rating: 4 Stars | **Category:** tool

HASHTAGS.ORG - http://hashtags.org

Tool which attempts to organize the world's hashtags. Provides hashtag analytics for your brand, business, product, service, event or blog. Input words that matter to you, and Hashtags looks to see the trends on Twitter.

Rating: 4 Stars | **Category:** engine

TWITTER HELP CENTER - https://support.twitter.com

Did you know Twitter has technical support? Yep, they do. It's relatively hidden, but here it is. It's more for users of Twitter, but it does have some juicy help for actual businesses on Twitter as well. Tweet, tweet, tweet.

Rating: 4 Stars | **Category:** resource

TWITAHOLIC - http://twitaholic.com

Tracks the most popular Twitter users based on followers. Use this to find top tweeters - sort of a top 100, 200, 300, etc list for the Twitterdom. Also just a great way to find out who's really famous on Twitter. Katy Perry, anyone?

Rating: 4 Stars | **Category:** service

TWITTER ANALYTICS - https://analytics.twitter.com

The official page for Twitter analytics and metrics. Sign up via Twitter, and learn how your tweets are doing!

Rating: 4 Stars | **Category:** tool

BITLY - https://bitly.com

Bitly is a URL shortening service that will track your click-throughs. Very useful for email marketing, blogging, and Twitter.

Rating: 4 Stars | **Category:** service

TWITTER FOR BUSINESS - https://business.twitter.com

Straight from the bird's mouth...learn how to use Twitter for business.

Rating: 4 Stars | **Category:** overview

IFTTT - https://ifttt.com

This app, If Then Then That, is a great tool for linking multiple social media accounts. It allows you to create 'recipes' that link your tools exactly the way you like them! For example: make a recipe that adds to a Google Apps spreadsheet every time a particular user uploads to Instagram - a great way to keep up with your competitors SMM strategies! With over 120 supported applications, the 'recipes' are endless, making this a good tool for your SMM strategies.

Rating: 4 Stars | **Category:** tool

LIKE EXPLORER - http://likeexplorer.com

Type in a URL and see its shares across social media outlets, including Facebook, Twitter, Google+, LinkedIn, Pinterest, and StumbleUpon. Very useful for link-building and competitor research.

Rating: 3 Stars | **Category:** tool

CROWDFIRE - http://crowdfireapp.com

Crowdfire is an interesting way to manage your relationships on both Instagram and Twitter (separately). With it, for example, you can manage fans (people who have followed you but whom you haven't followed), people who have recently unfollowed you, etc. Note: this tool requires Instagram/Twitter authorization for use with these social networks.

Rating: 3 Stars | **Category:** tool

CLICKTOTWEET - http://clicktotweet.com

ClickToTweet is a great way to encourage social sharing, especially of blog posts. Nudge your users to tweet your content.

Rating: 3 Stars | **Category:** tool

HOW TO USE TWITTER ON LINKEDIN -
http://help.linkedin.com/app/answers/detail/a_id/2754

What goes better than chocolate and peanut butter? LinkedIn and Twitter, of course. Start here to learn how to integrate Twitter on LinkedIn.

Rating: 3 Stars | **Category:** resource

TAGBOARD - http://tagboard.com

Hashtags started on Twitter, but now they are everywhere. Use this tool to research existing hashtags across a variety of social media, including Twitter, Facebook, Google+, Instagram, Flickr, Vine, and define your own. Fun and informative, too.

Rating: 3 Stars | **Category:** service

TWEET ARCHIVIST - http://tweetarchivist.com

Use this nifty service and tool to identify who is tweeting on your keywords and hashtags, and to analyze trends and data. In addition to Twitter, searches Instagram, Vine and Tumblr. Limited functionality for free, more with paid plans.

Rating: 3 Stars | **Category:** tool

TWITTER BLOG - http://blog.twitter.com

If Twitter is important to you, you should read this - the 'official' Twitter blog.

Rating: 3 Stars | **Category:** blog

TWIANGULATE - http://twiangulate.com

This nifty tool allows you to input up to three Twitter accounts. It then compares who follows each account and draws you a nifty map, plus identifies the most important followers, so you can see the 'network effect' of who follows whom on Twitter.

Rating: 3 Stars | **Category:** tool

TWITTER COUNTER - http://twittercounter.com

Use this Twitter application to find out how many people follow you, growth, and other metrics.

Rating: 3 Stars | **Category:** service

WHAT THE TREND - http://whatthetrend.com

What the Trend tracks trends on Twitter. So it's what is going viral, now, on Twitter. Mainly mainstream media stuff.. but you can use their search feature to find trends that interest you. Brought to us by HootSuite.

Rating: 3 Stars | **Category:** service

WHAT IS TWITTER - https://about.twitter.com/what-is-twitter

Twitter's infomercial site for individuals and businesses about what Twitter is, how it works, and how to get started.

Rating: 3 Stars | **Category:** resource

FOLLOWERWONK - https://followerwonk.com

This Twitter analytics tool will help you closely monitor your followers and influencers in your niche. It can help you find accounts, analyze your followers, and optimize your twitter activities for all your marketing needs. Brought to us by Moz.

Rating: 3 Stars | **Category:** service

SOCIALRANK - https://socialrank.com

If Instagram or Twitter are important to your business, you'll want to check out SocialRank. This tool provides analytics for both social networks (separately), in an easy to understand format. Instagram version isn't as multifaceted as the Twitter version, but both allow you to sort and filter your followers in many ways, including 'Most Valuable', 'Best Follower' and others. Note: this tool requires Instagram/Twitter authorization for use with these social networks.

Rating: 3 Stars | **Category:** tool

SUMALL - https://sumall.com

This free tracking service will help you aggregate and monitor your key business and social media stats. With more than 30 platforms to choose from, SumAll is adaptable to your marketing needs.

Rating: 3 Stars | **Category:** service

TWERIOD - http://tweriod.com

Tweriod gives you the best times to tweet. It analyzes both your tweets and your followers' tweets, so you can start tweeting when it makes most sense to reach others.

Rating: 3 Stars | **Category:** tool

TWITTERFEED - http://twitterfeed.com

Feed your blog to Twitter, Facebook, LinkedIn and other social networks, automagically.

Rating: 2 Stars | **Category:** service

GOO.GL - GOOGLE URL SHORTENER - http://goo.gl

Competitive with Bitly and Tinyurl comes Goo.gl - Google's official URL shortener.

Rating: 2 Stars | **Category:** tool